Milk and Tides

Also by Margaret Hasse:

Stars Above, Stars Below

In a Sheep's Eye, Darling

Milk and Tides

Margaret Hasse

NODIN PRESS

Cover drawing copyright © 2008, R.W. Scholes.

Book design and typeset: John Toren. Typeface: Bembo.

Grateful acknowledgement is made to the editors of the following publications in which some of these poems first appeared, occasionally with different titles:

33 Minnesota Poets, "Early Rusted Lilacs Send Us North"; *CALYX, A Journal of Art and Literature by Women,* "Forgetfulness in a Hardware Store When Seeking a Sillcock for an Outdoor Water Faucet"; *A View from the Loft,* "Little Pretty"; *Eating the Pure Light: Homage to Tom McGrath,* "On the Home Front"; *Minnesota Poetry Calendar 2000,* "First Day of Kindergarten"; *Poetry East,* "Big Hair," "Changing Voice," "Life in Reverse," "Living with Damage" and "The Mouth, Its Run"; *River Images,* "Yellowjackets"; *Touched by Adoption* and *Women's Lives, Women's Legacies,* "Marking Him"; *Water-Stone Review,* "Water Sign," "Winter Blessing," and "May 12, 2004: Twenty-Eighth Anniversary of My Mother's Death"; *What Light: This Week's Poem,* "In Response to the Evangelist Door-Knocking Who Asked: What Saves You?"

The lines from Part XIII "(Dedications)" from *An Atlas of the Difficult World,* copyright © 2002, 1991 by Adrienne Rich from *The Fact of a Doorframe: Selected Poems 1950-2001,* are used by permission of the author and W.W. Norton & Company, Inc.

Library of Congress Cataloging-in-Publication Data

Hasse, Margaret, 1950-
  Milk and tides : poems / Margaret Hasse.
      p. cm.
  Includes index.
  ISBN 978-1-932472-75-2
  I. Title.
  PS3558.A7255M55 2008
  811'.54--dc22

                                            2008014832

Nodin Press, LCC
530 North Third Street
Suite 120
Minneapolis, MN 55401

This book is for David.

CONTENTS

ACKNOWLEDGEMENTS

Thank you to the dear people who played roles in this book as readers, editors, enthusiasts, or advisors: Cris Anderson, Marge Barrett, Jill Breckenridge, Michael Dennis Browne, Ellen Buchanan, Marisha Chamberlain, Yvonne Cheek, Brigitte Frase, Sally French, Alex Grothe, Dave Grothe, Michael Grothe, Uve Hamilton, John Hasse, Mike Hazard, Sonjie Johnson, Merie Kirby, Patricia Kirkpatrick, Patrice Koelsch, Jim Lenfestey, Roseann Lloyd, Margaret Todd Maitland, Roy McBride, Amie Miller, Jim Moore, Ann Nelson, Rosa Maria de la Cueva Peterson, Tom Ruud, Richard Solly, Jon Spayde, and Lee Colin Thomas.

I received support for writing *Milk and Tides* poems from a National Endowment for the Arts Fellowship, a Loft-McKnight Fellowship, a Jerome Foundation Travel Grant, and writing residencies at Anderson Center for Interdisciplinary Studies, Blacklock Nature Sanctuary, Collegeville Institute for Ecumenical and Cultural Research, and Norcroft: a Writing Retreat for Women.

My heart is full of gratitude to Norton Stillman, Nodin Press publisher, with his fondness for many things, including Wordsworth's daffodils. My thanks also goes to John Toren, an associate of Nodin Press and a nimble maker of books. Becoming reacquainted with Randy Scholes and his amazing artwork confirms my faith in the endurance of creative spirit.

My sons appear in many of the poems, but with invented names.

                             – Margaret Hasse

↻ Prologue

The sea rises, the light fails, lovers cling to each other, and children cling to us. The moment we cease to hold each other, the sea engulfs us and the light goes out.

– James Baldwin, writer

In Response to the Evangelist Door-Knocking Who Asked: What Saves You?

Dusk doesn't, dawn does.
Morning splendor,
over and over and over again.
Newspapers don't, with their harpy
human interest stories.
But ah, coffee with milk in a plain white mug . . .

And graves in little cemeteries
in the country, on a hill, with a view.
It's good to think of spirits
having an eye for nature.

Sleep and dreams, the ones remembered,
even dreams about being chased because
that suspicion, that anxiety is given its
own body to run away.

Many books and almost every poem.

What saves often
comes right out of the blue:
a sudden glimpse from a bus
in crowded New York City –
a Lakota woman walking in a jingle dress.

Memory saves, especially random memory
that claims its own borders, its own orders,
makes its own metaphor.
A finger in an atlas seeking a town
on the west coast of Mexico
points to the face of a boy
selling candy on a bus a quarter-century ago
who couldn't talk, who moaned.

Going to work and coming back saves me.
On the Lake Street Bridge spanning the Mississippi,
a man's doing work for us all
waving his hand and his placard:
Support our troops — bring them home.
Honk in solidarity.

Dinner at home last night:
exhausted with meetings and money-making,
I sank into a chair at a table
where all the food was prepared
by my husband and lit by a candle:
salmon with basil and garlic,
deep green beans and a glass of wine.
Dave saying: *I'll rub your feet*
after dinner if you will just lie down
and put them in my lap.

The sight of my two sons saves me
even when they show me their backs.
Today that darkest month,
here in Saint Paul,
it's really cold, down
in the temperature teens.
My real-life teen heads off
to high school at 7 a.m. this morning,
coatless, gloveless, hatless,
his thick dreadlocks
all powdered with snow.

ʊ Milk

I know you are reading this poem as you pace beside the stove warming milk, a crying child on your shoulder, a book in your hand because life is short and you too are thirsty.

– Adrienne Rich, "(Dedications),"
An Atlas of the Difficult World

LATE HOUR IN AUGUST

A swath of wilderness
wraps our campfire,
a spark no satellite notices
in its dark registry of night.

Lying naked, we listen:
night noises, insect whine.
We talk over our life together
that I punctuate with exclamations.

You favor the question mark,
won't talk of endings, say:
See Perseus rising? Its brightest star
is 590 light-years away.

Meteors shower during
longer pauses in our conversation,
trailing ellipses . . .

I rest my hand on your damp thigh.
The pine tree's limbs outstretch
as if to catch flashes of light
that fall flame to ash,

gems of firelight, unkissed kisses.
Don't sleep, dear one, don't
leave me awake on this hard bed
with flares of desire, with thirst.

We don't have that much time.

The voyeuristic eye of a microscope peers
at a specimen where ooze from my body
holds my husband's active sperm
in its watery arms. The wetness is full of
ferns and smiley-face cells with whipping tails.
Very nice, the doctor says.

On a beach where horseshoe crabs couple
in secret, one soft-bellied, armored hand
cupped on top of the other, we lie nearby.
An hour before, we made love as a sliding
sheet of water pulled and pounded, surrounded,
receded, as if drawing us back to our beginnings.

The medical test reveals viscous,
high-quality mucus and sperm agile
as surfers on a board — but no answer
to why clinical perfection fails
to pass our urgent genetic message
on to the waves of the future.

We had named it in stunned anticipation
of late and hopeful parenthood, thinking

that it would answer to a name we gave,
Emily if a girl, Donald if a boy.

Even though, unknown to us, the life to come
was already spent; its heart beat a few times,

flickered out, and like a star's death
disclosed long after it passes away, we heard

its tiny, internal news from a doctor weeks later.
We had been taken in by the future:

looking at pictures in a pregnancy book,
week by week, we imagined

our grain of rice, our coffee bean,
our little curled fish.

The fantastic head would lift from its chest,
the spine grow straight as the ancient

amphibians came from the waters
to break the air with their breathing.

But it died a mass with tiny stumps
for arms when life looks like an amputee.

How to launch a spirit across the water
in its paper boat, birthday candles gone out?

GIVING BLOOD

Could I be a Good Samaritan
who kneels beside an accident victim,
tears a tourniquet off my shirt to bind a leg?
To the telephone appeal, *Won't you save
a life today by giving blood?* I say Yes.

After I offer my name, secure a date
at the blood bank, my heart sinks —
shots, needles, and nurses produce
chills and a thready pulse.
Years ago I donated cup after cup
to my mother's thirsty leukemia,
AB positive, our types matched.
Back then, eyes closed, I breathed deeply
as the pulse inside my arm pounded
and the plastic bag filled with beet-red blood.

I don't want to do it, I whine to my husband
who doesn't tease or advise cancellation.
Why don't I go instead? he offers.
Returned from my appointment he kept,
I feed him tenderloin steak, I rub his back,
I can not do enough for him.
He says*: Sweetheart, don't worry,
I'll always bleed for you.*

BASKET, RIVER

A baby placed
in a well-woven basket
of adoption
moves with the flow
that carries its little life
from one woman
to another whose arms
are ready to tend,
whose body has remained empty
of what she is in need of carrying,
who plucks the bundle
from among the bulrushes,
out of the stream.

I stand at the river,
thinking of the woman
upstream, how in the middle
of hardship and loss,
she had faith
in a small basket, a big river,
that someone with strong arms
would pull her beloved son
from the current, lift him high,
raise him to manhood,
the child of two mothers
who labored in different ways
believing in water's unbroken stream.

— for all women who have chosen
adoption for a child they bore

MARKING HIM

Does my little son miss the smell
of his first mother? I wonder
as the mewl of his mouth
opens toward a plastic bottle
that is not her breast.

Sudden new mother,
I bury my nose deep
into his skullcap of ringlets,
his starry cheesiness.

In her good-bye letter to him
sealed in his album
with a birth certificate, which now
lists my name as Mother,

his first mother writes
she nursed him briefly
after he emerged into
the second room of his world.

I think of milk, volcanic
and insistent, answering
the newborn's gigantic thirst,
a primal agreement between
generosity and greed.

Sometimes I press my nose
to the glass of that place
where a mother and my child
belong to each other;
I cannot imagine coming
between them.

But then I want to lick him all over
with a cow's thick tongue,
to taste him and mark him as mine
so if the other mother returns,
she will refuse her handled calf
smeared with my smell.

MILKY MOUTH

Wrapped in blue blankets
oh Baby Baby.

Skin smooth and brown egg color.
All ten fingers and all ten toes

plus three chins —
hey little Churchill.

Who are you in there?
What will you grow to be, russet potato

with so many eyes of sleep, all closed?
You hold a deep sleep patent.

Your sleep is a Precambrian layer,
a pecan dark in its shell.

You sleep like a bag of golden raisins.
Your sleep is a blessing boat

rocking in the bay.
White stars bloom over the village.

You arrived like a spark
aimed at the heart of wood,

like a love letter
addressed to our world, our avenue

to the two of us reading you
through the night.

Your cry casts a net,
draws us to you, little publican

of the nursery, dictator of
the changing table, of milk and tides.

You with damp curls
smell of dairy barns and talc,

whose soft skull will become helmet,
who will learn to roll over

like a small pooch.
You'll peek-a-boo happy as Houdini.

You will drop our hearts into
the river, padlocked in a cage

then rescue us again.
You will carry us to underground

rivers, to territories uncharted
when the earth was made.

What might appear in the cup of your hand?
A wild rabbit? A lick of rain?

In the broken eaves outside the nursery
sparrows, too, are nesting,

all feather and hope,
murmur and warm wings.

As we pick you up, sweet purple grape,
our arms wrap around you like vines.

You the flower, you the egg.
You the one who will fly.

Each day we discover a room in our house
we didn't know was there and you are in it, *Baby*.

TODDLER BOY BODY

One day he discovers his arms
useful for grabbing something
other than the floor, pulls himself
upright on the rungs of a chair.
The legs he employed to crawl
support him; the edge of a sofa
is his launching pad for first steps
astonishing as a moon walk.

After his bath, he wiggles away
from the rubdown of terrycloth,
giggling as if tickled, his bare
body packed with the sweet
chubbiness of infancy, which will
be carved away when he learns
to run — a troll on a diet.

Now, in his birthday suit of
warm brown skin, deep grooves
define his shape as if a tightly pulled
ribbon wrapped a soft package of clay
to create the curves of his buttocks,
the bulge of his tummy,
the pouch of his genitals.

Gradually, he'll retreat from
parading naked. Even in the bathtub,
he'll place a washcloth across his groin.
More of his flesh will become guarded,
his clothes cover the map of
his birthmark, the pit of his belly button.
His hidden body will be like
a sculpture viewed in a country
before the borders closed.

Deposed

With thousands of words at his disposal,
our three-year-old William, sovereign
of the house, loudly proclaims his opinions.
I don't like clothes with zippers or buttons,
he shouts one day as we help him dress.
I want a little family, just me with you two,
he insists as we try to warm him up
like cold milk to the idea of a sibling.

When William first peers into a green
blanket to find a new infant's face
like a fresh rosebud under petals,
he glares, then marches off like a soldier
to damage something — a siege
that beheads a vase of tulips.

Although we show room on our laps
for two children, William begs:
Put that baby down or send him back.
Back where? we ask.
To his birth mother, he replies. *Tell her*
we tried him out, and he didn't work.

From the kitchen monitor comes the sound
of baby Charlie cooing, then crying out sharply.
In the nursery, the unwilling older brother stands
crib-side, looking as if he'd like to kill
this tiny pretender to the throne.
His fingers are poised to pinch again.

Two-year-old Charlie loves water,

loves the force of water
in gutters, pipes, the second hose
bought to keep peace between brothers
who spray tomatoes with the intensity
of fire fighters at a five alarm fire,

loves the sources of water:
faucet, penis, rain, spit.

He longs like a pilgrim for wet places
where his worship is
complete submersion:
bathtub, swim pool, lake.

To praise water,
he secludes himself in the bathroom.
Ascending a stepping stool to the sink,
he opens valves to an endless rush
of new pressure in copper pipes.

So *much* water, why not share it?
Give it away until it seeps
through the floorboards,
showers into the kitchen,
fills the bowls on the table,
flows on the heads
of his amazed mother and brother
who do not immediately recognize
that grace might descend like this —
inconveniently —
from a complete enthusiast
who needs to be forgiven
for being generous
with whatever he loves.

FIRST DAY OF KINDERGARTEN

The bus steps are high, but William clambers up gamely.
Doors shut. He peers out a print-marked window.
From the street corner, I wave, wistful as a soldier's bride
as his bus pulls away and turns a corner.

At noon the yellow bus returns him
to the same place where I'm standing again.
He thinks I stood there all day, waiting in his absence.
When he finds out I left to play tennis,

his forehead crumples like paper in a wastebasket.
Now he knows I can move on my own without him.
Tears drawn from the well of desertion form in his eyes.
I'm his first love and his greatest disappointment.

In my dream, the ultrasound shows
the dark clot that is not a child
who would be six this summer.
Done with kindergarten,
her class picture might show
freckles, like mine, on the bridge
of her nose — faint stars that vanish
in the morning. No,

she was just a fistful of cells that stopped
going anywhere after the first trimester.
The doctor pointed to her image,
blighted nebula, the limits of her
disintegrating into a black hole.

Then the doctor scraped
and she was gone. But
would she have loved horses as I did,
dressing miniature palominos in saddles;
undressing them, letting them loose
on the carpet to caper and graze?

I cannot think of her for long as she negates
the possibility of my sons
who came through the determination
of adoption because we did not get her.

On opposite ends of a teeter-totter,
two kinds of children lift and descend.
On one seat, my never-never daughter.
On the other, two lively sons sit
on this side of life solid as stones,
catapulting her to the edge of thought.

THE MOUTH, ITS RUN

At three years old, Charlie stuttered badly,
a cold engine, hesitating, stalling.
His *Good morning* created a gaggle
of consonants so drawn-out his older brother

behind a citadel of cereal boxes at breakfast
asked: *Who taught him to talk like Porky Pig?*
I despised my students that year,
the ones who pierced their tongues,

hammered barbells through flesh,
sucked metal tacks on the roof
of their mouths, making slobber
and airy lisps on purpose,

while daily our blameless boy, sentenced
to the hard labor of language, his face
flushed with the effort of *Hello,*
chewed the cud of repeated sounds.

The speech therapist advised patience
with what can be a passing phase.
Don't finish his sentence.
Ignore his impediment.

Give the horse his head and he'll race free.
What was predicted came true.
Loose reins unleashed
the great gallop of speech.

AFTER I TELL FOUR-YEAR-OLD CHARLIE THE STORY OF HIS ADOPTION, HE COUNTERS WITH HIS OWN VERSION

When I was a baby fifty years ago,
when the dinosaurs all died of a heart attack,
there was no birth mother.
That's when I lived inside you, Mommy,
and came out of you —
the prettiest girl in the whole wild world.
And then I went to the hospital to get fixed.
Then I came home as a little guy on fast legs
and started running and having fun ha ha.

TOMATO WATCH

When it rains it looks like angels
are shooting bullets to the ground.

That wind we hear — where does it come from
and where does it go?

I'd like to be a garbage collector and get to hang out
on the back of the truck with one hand.

I will never ever get in a car with strangers,
not even if he gives me chocolick.

But did you know that we are strangers
to other people?

Do white people tell white lies
and black people tell black lies?

Why are we still down in the basement?
When will the tomato watch be over?

DISGUISES

The smoke of roasted pumpkin drifts down the street
from jack-o'-lanterns burning in the night.
A little ghost trips on his sheet and cries out.

A pint-sized pirate, an alien who lost his flashlight,
and a famous baseball player run from house to house.
Watchful parents on foot trail the trick-or-treaters.

My son's friend wanted to paint his face black
to complete his costume as Jackie Robinson.
My son's real skin would have restricted him

to the *colored section* just two generations ago.
My own face appears in the mask of a fake mother
to my hopped-up-on candy boy.

Yet I wear the worried look of any real mother
aware of ragged unlit pavement, tampered loot,
and the terrible whiteness of my own skin as we pass
a scarecrow hanging by his neck in a front yard.

Note Printed to His Father:
Sew Woof Bage on Cub Scot Unform

Badges — some boys
love to wear them
like birds banded
with bright colors.
Inside his uniform
William's shoulders
widen as in flight.

His father takes
the needle and thread
to the fabric of the badges,
stitching down the signs
of achievement and
pride and promises
our boy intends
to keep forever.

William cups his hand
when he covers his heart
as if he protects
a red butterfly there,
then touches each
of the eight emblems
on his blue shirt worn
with a yellow kerchief
and a napkin ring.

This morning my sixth grader with his broken hand,
like a bird dragging one wing, perches on the bed,
watches me in my Greet-the-Sun ritual.
I face east toward a wall that lacks a window, but has
                                    a lamp.
He asks: *Is the light bulb your fake sun?*

He reminds me again that I am his *fake mother*,
and that he forgives his birth mother
because he thinks if he were with her, he would
                                    be poor,
in a family with ugly cars. *I might be a jailbird*, he says.

I breathe slowly — where does he get these notions?
I move out of the downward dog posture, into the
                                    inclined plane,
the bent knee pose, curved back, opposite lunge,
                                    Uttanasana,
then become a mountain, Tadasana. There, welcome day.

Yoga helps me find patience with the chaos
of my incessantly impatient boy, at breakfast chanting
now now now, gimme gimme gimme like a magpie
while waffles brown and rise in their neat metal
                                    squares.

He continues in the stream-of-consciousness way
                                    he has,
darting about, pecking at ideas, chirping:
Black people like me get so patient because
we have to learn to wait for the bus to come.
Where is that deep lake of quiet and calm, the one
at the back of my mind I meditate toward?
Today, it's a puddle evaporating into a hot, difficult day.

MAY 12, 2004: TWENTY-EIGHTH ANNIVERSARY OF MY MOTHER'S DEATH

My mother strokes my hair, pulls
a strand behind my ear. I wake
to heavy rain on the roof as if our house
were a toy washed under a waterfall.

At breakfast I tell my son that
I was with my mother when she died.
He asks how dying is,
and whether we die once,
the way we live once.
I could not answer, having just lost
my mother again in my dream.

I turn my wet face
to show my son — what?
If I were honest, I would say
I want him to see how deeply
he will miss me.

I would say sometimes
there is little we can do
for our children but go on living.
To be a tree in the rain for my son
to lean his whole nature against
until he knows how real he is
when I am gone.

For two weeks Scrubbers,
my son's hamster, has been dying,
her breathing slow.

Abandoned now,
the little Ferris wheel,
the plastic tubes she slid through.

I lift her light body
in the cup of my hand
thinking to warm her.

She bites down hard,
draws blood from my finger
reminding me that my father

in the agony of his long death
attacked his family with words.
In the hospital, when we urged

him to sit up, he spat out:
You can't make me happy,
so that we'd leave him alone

with the right to his own death
and not the death
we thought he should have.

Staked out on a chain, the dog Penny
pushes her copper-colored nose
into the cold wind to learn
all the news the air will carry.
Baited by a squirrel's smell,
she profiles the broad skull
that made the vet sigh: *pit bull.*

Let loose, Penny might chase down
and damage a deer, a dog, a ball, a child.
Therefore: rope, muzzle, cage,
constant vigilance.
In her troubled past, homeless
and broken by blows,
Penny ate garbage and road kill.
Now we drag her from gobbling
scat that peppers the ground.

Her insecurity and poor vision often
make me a stranger. When I wear a hat,
she advances full-bore, growling.
When sense of smell or sight
registers FRIEND, abruptly she halts,
topples on her haunches,
sheepishly slobbers my hands.

Through Penny, I learn how trust —
hurt and angry — still lays daily claim
to a crazy fierce tenderness
on the rough terrain of love.
On the day when my son
gouges holes in the window screens,
then asks: *We'll never give up on her,
will we, whatever she does?*

I put my arms around him,
saying *never, never, never*
pounding the words forcefully
like a stake deep into ground.

CHANGING VOICE

Because he is only thirteen, his anger
flares, a gassed fire.

Because he is only thirteen, he snarls like a cur,
dislikes everything about his parents,

especially what they like,
books they read, jokes they tell.

Because his voice trips and falls,
as if on a loose rug, he breaks into tears.

Because the salt caves in the pits
of his arms are newly rank, he locks

himself in the bathroom for a hot
shower, steams paper from the wall.

Because he is small for his age,
he disparages his brother's thighs

carried by those long bones:
You're flabby, he screams, dangling

upside down like a bat from
the upper berth of their bunk bed.

Because he struggles to read
when others kids are quick

to spit words from their mouths,
he runs as if to surpass the wind

on a windy day, bedtime on a summer day,
chores and studying and rules every day.

Because he is only thirteen, sometimes
he still curls in his mother's arms,

grubbing for stories he stars in:
how he could climb from his crib

to claim his own baby bottle,
how he's graded A+ in music

for notes his trumpet hangs high
like the sound of wild birds

over the heads of other kids
who can't believe he's only thirteen.

HOMEWORK

Six foot one, *and still he grows*
portends the pediatrician studying
an X-ray with my boy's plates
still un-fused, milky millimeters apart.
Now that I look way up at him,
my authority over his bedtime shrinks.

Ripe as a plum, his skin is not so
dark as to cover blemishes —
a dash of pimples across his cheek
and a single blackhead,
tiny tack at the tip of his nose.
I'm itching to pop it! — squeeze
the dirt out with my fingernails,
grooming like a mama baboon.
The very idea would gross him out,
as in *totally*.

How to give up the job I know totally
of reminding him to brush his teeth,
of braiding his hair in corn rows,
of dancing with him as I did
when he learned the two-step
wearing his first suit and tie.

What he lets me do now is provide
food and homework help as long as
I stay on my side of the table.

The Military Recruiter Calls Eleven Times during Dinner

> *And if it's a boy he'll carry a gun,*
> *sang the crow on the cradle.*
>
> — from a traditional song
> popularized by Jackson Browne

1.
Please, we are eating now.

2.
This time, we ignore the ringing phone.

3.
When my son does
pick up the receiver,
he's polite at first,
speaks between
long pauses:
Yes, I like sports.
Yes, I like travel.
Yes, I want money.
Then he is silent.
No, not now.
Then he hangs up.

4.
Let me describe how my son's face
darkens with his five o'clock shadow.
Air through a screen door
carries the green message of spring.
Let him enjoy his meal here at home.

5.
Wrong number,
wrong, wrong, wrong.

6.
Papery sounds
of a large bird's wings
flap around the house.
The bird perches
on the rooftop, drapes
wings of crepe
across the windows.

7.
You are a hearse of feathers.
You descend like oil over the road.
You tack a corsage of blood
on a dead rabbit.
I run at you screaming.

8.
Please, come over to our house,
let me give you supper.
My boy is out somewhere, but
show me your scars, let me act
a Scheherazade, with a heart full
of stories about my boy.

9.
Here, see for yourself he's very young.
He still sleeps with Bunny, a stuffed animal,
worn down with tenderness and need
to only a head, one eye,
a stringy tendon attached to a dirty foot
looking like a body blown to bits.

10.
Hell no, he won't go.

11.
Your pencil has a sharp tooth,
grown man, a big mouth
gobbling up the names
of boys who haven't voted,
haven't made love.
Some are not citizens.
You ask them to hand over
a life before it's theirs to give.

BIG HAIR

This fall, our son's chosen
to grow his hair out long.

He keeps his tresses clean,
otherwise lets the fields lie fallow,

doesn't cultivate with comb and brush.
One woman stares so long at our boy's

hair, she trips over the curb.
Our mellow teen's unfazed,

but his friend shouts at her:
Why don't you just take a picture?

In winter, ropey knots and dreadlocks
raise a lion's mane around his face.

On myspace.com, he uses Bob
Marley's photo, not his own.

Now in hot spring, he scores his first job,
can't fit his 'do into the employee cap,

decides to have the wild bush
whacked, but declines the barber

whose shop attracts other young
black men with high style.

There's no escape for his father
who pulls out hair-trimming tools

inherited from his grandma.
William drapes a Batman cape,

sits on a kitchen stool so his dad can shear
the black mats that fall like Brillo pads.

The one now bald doesn't appear
to be the same boy: a soldier

could wear this chiseled head.
But look again, a soft-hearted youth

comes back thinking how to use
the surplus he raised and leaves behind.

Could it make a wig? he asks,
for someone like your mother

who got sick? I mask a smile,
imagine setting on her bare head

an ebony Rastafarian crown, bold
as shining gold bequeathed

from a grandson
she would have loved to hold.

ↄ Tides

Help us to be the always hopeful
Gardeners of the spirit
Who know that without darkness
Nothing comes to birth
As without light
Nothing flowers.

– May Sarton, "The Invocation to Kali"

WHAT IT IS LIKE FOR ME THIS FALL

This fall joints swell with dry heat when the furnace
comes on. I wake up hot and flushed, cast off clothes,
then shiver until the sun comes up.
I sweat and kick the covers, sweat, and then cool,
rowing across menopause,
death at my back.

I'm remembering the therapist who said years ago:
You will be happier if you think more about death,
and if you let your body eat whatever it wants.

This fall my husband snores softly, and
softly, I pet him so he will roll over
and relax his throat.

This fall the 2,000th soldier died in Iraq,
a man with a name his mother chose.

My younger son breaks his hand. With only one
working hand — whoosh — he reverts to being a
      toddler.
He can't zip his own zipper, can't tie his own shoes.
His trumpet sleeps in its baby casket case.

This fall I think: how did it happen,
to have a child demanding so much support
when my own body requires extra care,
a stiff neck without a swan's bend,
knees fat and rubbery, and a need
to wake three times in the night to pee?
I am dream-famished from troubled sleep.

This fall I am so big to my boys
they need to belittle me —
my memory, my math, my skill at tennis — all are bad,
are *lame. You never took advanced algebra,* they accuse.
But I did! Even though I never use it now.

This fall I think: you never know your last period
has come and gone, until it never comes again.

*— after Deborah Keenan's
"What It Was Like Today" poems*

DREAMING OF A THIRSTY BIRD

To the thirsty bird, I carry water,
write my mother an endless
thank-you letter as I surface
from sleep to relearn
my mother is long dead.
I'm aged forty years
in the flash of waking up
to the top of another cycle
of chores that can't be shirked:

breakfast for the boys,
homework help,
and a toilet requiring
a plunger and a snake.

When I was eight, I had
a canary who fluttered
like an origami blossom
within its cubic foot of flight.
One hot week of summer,
I forgot to hook the glass cups
of water, like ears, to its cage.
Nothing heard it die of thirst.
It's my fault, I sobbed over
the riffraff of feathers, but then
a spasm in my gut let loose
a hiccup's happy cork:

no longer would I need
to change dirty newspapers.
I could hunker down
on Saturday's luxurious couch
and carelessly read all day.

In a scrapbook of family recipes,
this margin note: *Better with churned butter.*
What wouldn't be?
A grey Midwestern day would be better
served with sun.

Today, I am baking
with canned fruit
and store-bought crust
remembering how the story goes:
my uncles back from World War II
put themselves in danger again
for homemade apple pie
that shattered in a hot glass plate.

Their wives tried to stop them,
but were also proud of that much
hunger in their husbands
who gummed the mash
to strain shards, then ate it all,
insisting: *men died for this.*

MILK FROM CHICKENS

The day my son declared with hammerhead certainty
that milk comes from chickens was the day
I yanked him out of the city
and drove west to farm and prairie land.

Like a nail pried from hard wood, he complained
from the back seat, missing electronic games and TV.
Near the South Dakota border, he saluted
a McDonald's as we flew by.

I wanted my boy to take a turn lifting
barb wire to slip into open fields
keeping an eye out for the crazy bull.
I wanted him to hold a bottle for a lamb,

to feel the fierceness of animal hunger,
the suck of an animal mouth.
I wanted him to sleep in darkness encoded
with urgent messages of fireflies,

to see the bright planets in alignment overhead,
to stand on the graves of his grandparents,
dead so many years before he was born,
and to trace the names etched on granite pillows,

hard as the last sleep.
How else to plant in him the long root of plains grass,
help him reach water in drought and
know who his mother is?

The land doesn't know you've been gone.
West of the river at Rosebud, the road rises toward
buttes,
    then sighs down to a creek bed
        where red willows bunch.
Flocks of birds muster in the sky along one blade of
wind,
    fall to pieces over a field
        of black calves and their grazing mothers.
One cow looks up with her slaughter-house face,
    a muzzle of mist,
        enormous wet eyes.

High grass of the ranch land bows down to the breeze.
The weather in the west — grey, carping clouds — is
        half a day distant.
You fill up with sun and sky; your head becomes
        big and solemn as a sunflower.
You read everything contained
        between the covers of four directions.

A Breeze Bends the Grasses

the kind my father picked
and brought to his lips to blow
the sound of a startled bird —

the cry his heart must have made
when he drove himself far
from us time and again.

Teach me, teach me
to make music
from plain grass.

Father showed me the way
to stretch a blade between thumbs,
to whistle a lone note.

He said: *That's it! Good,*
coaching me to climb a scale,
hit high notes,

practicing a melody
of happiness
he could not compose.

Why did I think all these years
only of how he was distant,
then disappeared,

and not of how he placed
his hands around mine
praying with me a green song?

FOUND IN MY MOTHER'S BUDGET BOOK

A dried blossom thin
as tissue paper dropped
from a budget book
belonging to Mother.
An aster maybe, the color
too drained to discern.
Petals overlap
like clasped hands.
In the ledger she kept,
line after line
of worried digits
crouch as if the pen
were mean with ink.
Each expense noted:
10¢ for eggs
25¢ — cotton shirt
$1 to pull a tooth.
Outlay must agree
with narrow income.

After a close winter,
after a cool spring,
finally in summer
we went walking
in country ditches
in sandy fields
everywhere in Dakota.
For free, we vased
raffish pink roses,
took a teacup of
common blue violets,
poked oxeye daisies
into a tin can —
extravagance
anyone could afford.
Small wonder she saved
a wildflower
to balance the chart
of our accounts.

BLUE

*Soir de Paris or Evening in Paris started to be sold in the
1920s as an inexpensive perfume. By the 1950s, it was touted
as "the fragrance more women wear than any other in the
world," yet by 1969 it had disappeared.*

A woman in her periwinkle cotton housedress lies
on a sagging sofa with a piece of Scotch tape pressed
onto the furrows between her eyes to flatten wrinkles.
Six children, two in diapers, buzz around her like blue
flies she must brush away in order to nap, in order to
keep from crying. She is so tired, she dreams of a blue
baby lost under a stone lamb. This same woman rises
refreshed with her violet blue eyes and a new soft blue
velvet in her voice, to let her oldest daughter select
for her a dressy dress, watch as she touches a finger to
the cobalt blue lips of a bottle: Evening in Paris *eau
de toilette* (a phrase that makes her children giggle).
On the nape of her neck hidden by hair, on the wrist
where the veins run blue under the delta of her skin,
her flesh feels metallic blue and so cool, she shivers
in the August heat. Carrying a pocketbook, wearing
lipstick, she takes the arm of her husband in his Navy
uniform. They step out into blue dusk pulling down
its shade over the Missouri River. They step out for an
evening in South Dakota.

This morning, blue with a hint of rain,
I think of you.
For the mornings you were alive
and here among us,
I thank you.

Could I have loved mornings more
when you were alive
than right now, when I am alive
and know that some day
I will follow you?
Could I have loved you more
when you had breath in your mouth,
and the thin tissue of skin
wrapped around your body?

Each time I remember you,
I want to make me better.
I can't of course. I'm stuck then, like a star
in the black firmament of a child's drawing,
and you, too, you dear dead one
who burned out years ago,
your light still arriving here on earth.

MEADOWLARK: MENDING SONG

What hurt you today
was taken out of your heart
by the meadowlark
who slipped the silver needle
of her song
in and out of the grey day
and mended what was torn.

My friend has too many possessions
in her small apartment. They impede her ch'i.
Stacks of papers provoke asthma, records
of her first book prevent new writing.
She's getting rid of stuff, explaining: *I'm at the stage*
of life I don't add more things, I have to simplify.

I'm not ready for simple.
Even though I own a shelf sagging with books
about Feng Shui, about managing clutter,
I still welcome other people's giveaways.

My friend and I are about the same size.
If we were scrappy shoppers and she still thirsty
for things, we might squabble over
the same black dress on the ten rack.
When she spills her excess on the table —
jewelry tossed like magic dice,
I try on everything at the same time,
thinking of women in Korea who wore
valuables on their ears, their fingers,
banking on their bodies safer than houses.

My friend says that the woman who made
these cobalt blue earrings wants a child —
I'll wear them and think: *fly home, little bird.*
The pearl necklace came from my friend's attorney
who walked her through the burned fields of divorce.
I'll wear it and remember: *green grass of new love.*

I take on what she gives away.
Just now, I'm wearing her blue shirt.
I breathe in and she breathes out.
Can she take the rest she needs right now

if I keep her clothes busy for a while?
My hands reach from her shirt cuffs
to touch things with kindness
and generosity, to be like the soft
and long-fingered hands of my friend.

– for Roseann Lloyd

Sometimes we're drawn close by a stranger
as if in the presence of someone

we used to know who returns to us like water
dipped and poured into a new vase.

Who was the guppy before she ogled us from the
        aquarium?
Perhaps the child who used to round her mouth and
        say *oh.*

And what if souls inhabit things beyond people and
        animals? —
In the yellow rose bush, my mother blooms again.

We might revisit the world as a rag to shine
the loafers of travelers recycling through time.

The brown of the shoe used to color a calf.
I'd rather be a leather purse than a shoe occupied
        by a foot.

A handbag holds a tube of lipstick endowed
by a spirit that presses its pink on a woman's mouth

until its reaches its end, vanishes
to become something else —

a cottonwood tree, a safety pin,
a wooden gate pushed open by its old companion,
        the wind.

LITTLE PRETTY

A bluster of wind knocked the house around.
This morning, we learn the basswood tree
was yanked from its roots like a giant tooth.
Cyclones damage, but in my mind's eye
Dorothy and Toto swirl away.

What if we could ride the currents of air
with birds and land unscathed in places
present or past, twisting time?
My beautiful friends watch *The Wizard of Oz*,
drink dry martinis and mimic all the words.
Michael cackles: *I've got you my little pretty.*
Gary does Dorothy's *No place like home*,
making click-click sounds with his mouth
as the heels of his tennis shoes touch.

A tornado spirals down on another scene.
Sick green goes with the storm before it hits.
Michael in his hospital bed tittering: *Darling,*
just look at my skin, such a bizarre shade of green.
Absolutely nothing in my closet goes with green.
Deep green goes with a tree that cracks and falls
as the winds pass through and on.

August, the avid yellowjacket wasps
cling to whatever remains
on the picnic table: wine bottles, Coke cans.
They circle places where children eat and spill.
They buzz in the caves of dented Kool-Aid cups.
They land, many legged, aggressive.
They are dying, we're told, eager to cling
to any sweetness, like humans who know
they will die soon, who pour over papers,
stare at photographs, want their hair brushed.
My mother begged for perfume
to cover her medicinal smell
when the doctor came around.

The children attack the wasps, waving napkins.
The insects dive-bomb back.
The men joke about revenge on insects,
boast of bare legs.
Stoic Nora Rose allows a wasp
to crawl like a sealed kiss
on the contract of her lips.
Where has she learned – so young – reserve
in the face of harm?

The Dog Star comes out.
We sit in a sac of coolness.
The first fall leaves tell
their whispery stories of dry loss.
The wasps disappear.
Everyone stays late at the party placing
the last sugar of summer on our tongues.

WINTER BLESSING

Snow saddles the palomino ponies
which the cold jockey
of winter rides.
One dowdy old mare
wears an uncurried undercoat.
She nudges broken bales of hay,
chews placidly, her teeth
pegged like piano keys.

When I enter the paddock
as a woman dissolving
into the grey landscape
of middle age,
she lifts her long face to show
the coal of curiosity
and the white crescents
of doubt in her eyes.

From a grave stillness,
her whole body startles.
Rotating on a back hoof,
she aims toward the open gate.
She bucks, blasts gas
and flashes the willow switch
of her tail reminding me
of the spunk a girl needs
to grow old.

EARLY RUSTED LILACS SEND US NORTH

Disappointed when the lilacs
rusted so quickly this spring,
we started to see ourselves,
my friend and I, as women
of grey-streaked hair with whom
only the old butcher flirts.

Driving tired into the cooler
north of Minnesota, we
discover masses of lilacs
just beginning to bloom
blue, white, a purple profusion
like rain clouds rolling up
the sleeve of the horizon.

The bushes call us from our
car; we stand in the ditch,
our shoes wet with forgiving
dew, and break big branches
in a rough hungry way,
laying the stolen flowers
on newspapers in the back seat —
like shards of lavender stars
that grant wishes — or sparklers
which we as children used
to write our names in the dark.

– for Patricia Kirkpatrick

FORGETFULNESS IN A HARDWARE STORE
WHEN SEEKING A SILLCOCK
FOR AN OUTDOOR WATER FAUCET

We need a plumbing part at ACE —
I forget the technical name, retaining
less about more things as the tides
of my age turn, dragging information
like broken glass beyond
the barrier reef of recall.

The term I'm trying to bring to mind
contains genital slang and is sibilant
so I try hissing.
I picture using the item, imagine
watering hydrangea with big blue heads
like a bouquet of elderly women.

The rainless summer had wilted the pine.
The spigot needs this object to work.
To jumpstart memory through motion,
I pretend to turn the tiny pilot's wheel.

The clock knows time is passing — tick tock.
Memory loves a rhyme. The word pops up
like a crocus. Jot it down: *Sillcock!*
The hardware store now holds joy
fresh as a new patent.
For a price, I carry away
a small silvery noun. *Sillcock.* Necessary
to satisfy the world's thirst to be remembered.

In the pale night, black and white dairy cows
lumber from the meadow to congregate by the fence,
grinding the grist mills of their jaws,
going over and over and over what they have.
My friend and I are momentary companions of animals,
the milky moon, and Venus high in the western sky.
A pinpoint of pink light — that's Jupiter
rising to the occasion of June, which breaks
the next morning clear and blue and bugless.

Now dew polishes the grass to glitter.
Sheared wool mulches the tomato plants.
Lambs persist in calling for their mothers.
We sit still so long the barn cats
trust us with their lives in our laps.
The hummingbird sticks her needled beak
far into the columbine's paper lantern.
Finches flash like goldfish of the air
above the pasture that rolls out
a green carpet down to the creek.
Waiting to be relieved of their milk,
cows lower their heads as humans do
when they pray, humbled by burdens.

Patient, the flared bells of rhubarb plants.
Patient, the asparagus that takes years
to establish its patch, then escapes from the yard
to live in ditches with wild plum bushes.
And who wouldn't risk running away
to take a branch of white blossoms
in your arms, to smell the precious
scent of a brief, starry blooming?

KEEP UP YOUR STRENGTH, COUSINS SAY

1.
At a routine physical, the young doctor explains
that the new click in my old knee joint
with the cartilage worn away
has the creepy name of crepitus.
I tell her the age lines around my lips hurt
the way years ago my jaw ached
after big parties when I grinned too much.
Eat, keep up your strength! my South Dakota cousins say.
Now food brings lethargy, not renewal.
Is this the age I start to become my grandmother,
when my arms soften to rice pudding,
freckles rise into shapes like raisins
and I hitch up those lowered breasts?
Hey! I say to myself, you're not there yet.
Make yourself last long like a popsicle.

2.
In aging, there is no strength in numbers:
my husband stands on the household scale
for the first time in twenty years staring down
bewildered at how time has piled it on.
He rubs the half-dollar tonsure of thinned hair on his head.
His eyebrows have grown in a wild scarecrow way.
And what about those amazingly stubby hairs
on my own chin, plucked, then popped out again
overnight like bottle brushes?
My husband complains he must be looking
old to his fellow teachers — the young women
at his elementary school see him nearing retirement,
step over him like a sidewalk crack,
adopt a new textbook without his opinion.

3.
We're growing old! How did we not see it coming?
Other people are fooled by us, too.
Somebody we haven't seen in a while
almost doesn't recognize us at a grocery store,
says our names with a question mark, and stares until
our familiar faces surface out of the murky water
of older, greyer, bespeckled features,
and are welcomed, with relief.

4.
Young people look past us as if at a clock
and see us only as part of a collection of older people
who did something once that was impressive.
Now, we're a little scary in our zeal to put ourselves
out in the world, teach, have opinions, take
long walks, monopolize the good tables in coffee shops.
To stay abreast of *The New York Times*,
we read vociferously, complete the crossword puzzle,
drink energizing coffee and steamed milk trying
to keep our strength up.

ॐ Epilogue

I am not done with my changes.

– Stanley Kunitz, from "The Layers"

LIFE IN REVERSE

What if life were designed for us to arrive
when we're ancient, then grow younger?
If we start out as elders in our eighties
or nineties and change toward youth,
when our knees start working again
like well-oiled latches to a gate,
we do not protest grey hair or difficult digging
in the ragbag of memory for the right word.

When we become seventy years old, we're elated
that our bodies are as spry as they are
for we've passed down from real decrepitude.
We know what old age hath wrought —
disabilities, diapers, disease.
That's over now and we look forward
to decades of vitality.

We enter our sixties, that marvelous epoch
of activity, when we are now known
for something, when people see us as fluid,
not finished with our changes.
The driver's license we relinquished is back
in our hands. We take only occasional naps,
are into long walks, road trips and good works.
We have decent teeth and foods agree with us.

Our fifties — a really dreamy time.
Lovemaking is not an effort anymore.
Our flesh, though somewhat loose,
is more elastic than it used to be.
We cherish the work we do, whatever it is —
making things, going to meetings —
because we didn't get to do these things
back when we were eighty.
When stuck on the freeway,
we sing along to the radio.

When we grow back to forty,
we wear tighter, shorter clothes.
We can't get enough of color and travel.
As we build new rooms in our life,
we work on being generous because
we recall our old age when we appreciated
visitors at the nursing home, even if
they were the sons of the neighbors' son.

Thirty, we're ecstatically thirty,
even with our struggles.
Maybe the marriage isn't ideal,
and we have to move a few times, but
it's all experience, experience, and we thrive
on our power to learn.

In our twenties, we look down at our bodies
amazed how they shine with youth,
the flesh springy and firm
like a forest floor under pine trees.
We like sex outside, or on a table.
We welcome work and opportunities.

Next comes adolescence, which
used to be the best and worst of times,
because we felt so much
and knew so little.
But our past maturity gives
our teenage years ballast.
Now it's only the best of times.
We consistently make great decisions,
learn to play the flute,
show kindness to ourselves and our parents.
We are avid about education, use birth control,
enjoy in every way our glory.

When we get into grade school,
the great sex we used to have
when we were older is now
yucky to even think about.
Our parents tower over us.
Candy tastes delicious.
Nothing could be better
than playing kick-ball all afternoon.
We love our mother's voice
murmuring, her perfume,
the way stars are brighter
than they've ever been.
We can fall asleep anywhere
opening our hearts to dream,
and we wake up smaller,
believing in the stories
where animals talk.

And then we are losing language,
but playing with all the toes on our feet.
Someone is usually holding us
and it feels so good to suck.
When we slide into the birth canal,
there's an agreeable sensation
of being drawn from a place
big and bright that often made us cry
into a cozy padded cave
where we rest with our ears
pressed to the pulse of a universe.
Then we are stilled with a lullaby
before lullabies had sound.

INDEX

About the Author

Margaret Hasse, originally from South Dakota, lives in Saint Paul, Minnesota, with her husband and two sons. At Stanford University (B.A.) and the University of Minnesota (M.A.), she majored in English. Her previous collections of poetry are *Stars Above, Stars Below*, New Rivers Press, 1984, winner of the Minnesota Voices competition, and *In a Sheep's Eye, Darling*, Milkweed Editions, 1988, winner of the Lakes and Prairies competition and a finalist for a Minnesota Book Award.

Among the poetry anthologies including her work are: *Thirty-Three Minnesota Poets*, Nodin Press, 2000; *Sisters of the Earth*, Vintage Books, 1991 and 2003; *To Sing Along the Way: Minnesota Women Poets from Pre-Territorial Days to the Present*, New Rivers Press, 2006; and *Where One Voice Ends, Another Begins: 150 Years of Minnesota Poetry*, Minnesota Historical Society Press, 2007.